Celebrating
Hispanic
Diversity

THE PEOPLE
AND CULTURE OF
MEXICO

Rachael Morlock

PowerKiDS press.

New York

Published in 2018 by The Rosen Publishing Group, Inc.
29 East 21st Street, New York, NY 10010

First Edition

Editor: Theresa Morlock
Book Design: Rachel Rising

Photo Credits: Cover, iStockphoto.com/Steve Debenport; Cover (background) Alija/E+/Getty Images; Cover, p. 1 https://commons.wikimedia.org/wiki/File:Flag_of_Mexico.svg; p. 5 tateyama/Shutterstock.com; p. 7 BorisVetshev/Shutterstock.com; p. 9 StanislavBeloglazov/Shutterstock.com; p. 11 JONATHAN NACKSTRAND/AFP/Getty Images; p. 13 Morenovel/Shutterstock.com; p. 15 Suriel Ramzal/Shutterstock.com; p.17 Cristina Stoian/Shutterstock.com; p. 19 Gerardo C.Lerner/Shutterstock.com; p. 21 https://commons.wikimedia.org/wiki/File:Aztec_codex_replica.jpg; p. 23 Lena Wurm/Shuttterstock.com; p. 25 Kobby Dagan/Shutterstock.com; p. 27 Ingrid Deelen/Shutterstock.com; p. 29 Anton_Ivanov/Shutterstock.com; p. 30 Brothers Good/Shutterstock.com.

Library of Congress Cataloging-in-Publication Data
Names: Morlock, Rachael.
Title: The people and culture of Mexico / Rachael Morlock.
Description: New York : PowerKids Press, 2018. | Series: Celebrating hispanic diversity | Includes index.
Identifiers: ISBN 9781538327067 (pbk.) | ISBN 9781508163107 (library bound) | ISBN 9781538327500 (6 pack)
Subjects: LCSH: Mexico–Juvenile literature. | Mexico–Social life and customs–Juvenile literature.
Classification: LCC F1208.5 A73 2018 | DDC 972–dc23

Manufactured in the United States of America

CPSIA Compliance Information: Batch #BW18PK: For Further Information contact Rosen Publishing, New York, New York at 1-800-237-9932

CONTENTS

WHAT DOES "MEXICAN" MEAN?

What does it mean to be Mexican? Some Mexicans trace their roots to **Mesoamerican** civilizations that flourished hundreds of years ago. Others connect to traditions created during the 300 years of Spanish colonization, beginning in 1521. Mexico continued to change after becoming an independent country in 1821. Today, most Mexicans have both Mesoamerican and Spanish ancestors. They are called mestizos.

Like its people, the culture of Mexico is **diverse**. It's a rich blend of the many voices, stories, artistic forms, foods, **rituals**, and beliefs of Mexicans throughout history. Today, 122 million people live in this country where traditional and modern cultures are colorfully combined and people of all backgrounds come together as Mexicans.

The Plaza de las Tres Culturas in Mexico City was named for the Mesoamerican, Spanish, and mestizo cultures that its buildings represent.

5

A VARIED LANDSCAPE

Mexico lies between the Pacific Ocean and the Gulf of Mexico and shares borders with the United States, Belize, and Guatemala. It's made up of large mountain ranges, deep valleys, dry deserts, snowcapped volcanoes, steamy rainforests, and beautiful beaches.

These **environments** provide homes for many plants and animals. Jaguars, anteaters, spider monkeys, and tropical birds live in the rainforests, while marine creatures, such as gray whales, swim along the coasts. More than 100 kinds of cacti grow in the desert. Natural resources are abundant and include oil, silver, copper, gold, and lead.

In different areas of Mexico, there are different types of wildlife that can survive in the climate there. However, pollution and **deforestation** threaten this land and its **biodiversity**.

Ik-Kil is a cenote near Chichén Itzá in Mexico. A cenote is a natural well or sinkhole that exposes the groundwater underneath.

Monarch Migrations

Mexico's location between the Arctic Circle and the equator provides perfect conditions for creatures seeking a warmer winter home through **migration**. Monarch butterflies fly south from Canada and the United States every year, covering thousands of miles on their journey. When they reach the mild mountain valleys of Michoacán, Mexico, and other parts of the country, their fluttering black, orange, and white wings transform the landscape. Between 30 million and 100 million monarch butterflies breed in Michoacán each year before flying north again.

MESOAMERICAN PEOPLES

The first residents of Mexico probably traveled over a land bridge from Asia and along the North American coast before settling in Mexico. Over generations, civilizations such as the Olmec, the Aztecs, the Maya, and the Toltec developed. Though different, they shared practices such as ritual **sacrifices**, careful study of the stars, and the creation of ranked social groups. They built cities and pyramids and learned to understand and shape the world around them through agriculture, mathematics, art, and religion.

The descendants of these cultures are the Mesoamerican people who make up 14 percent of the Mexican population. Mesoamerican communities value family and tradition and speak languages that have been used since **pre-Hispanic** times, before the introduction of the Spanish language. Elements of Mesoamerican arts, **customs**, and history are powerful symbols of Mexican identity.

The Pyramid of the Sun is one of the largest pyramids in the world. The Aztec people used incredible skill and organization to construct it in the ancient city of Teotihuacán.

9

HEROES AND HISTORICAL FIGURES

Mexican culture celebrates individuals who took a stand to protect their community. One early Mexican hero is Cuauhtémoc, an Aztec emperor who defended the city of Tenochtitlán from the Spanish conqueror Hernán Cortés. Despite his defeat, Cuauhtémoc's strength is legendary.

Under Spanish rule, brave Mexicans spoke out against unjust colonization. In 1810, the priest Miguel Hidalgo y Costilla began a rebellion by ringing church bells and calling for a free and independent Mexico. His courage led others to join the movement, which ended in 1821. Years later, in 1910, the Mexican people rose against the *Porfiriato*, or the Porfirio Díaz dictatorship; the Mexican Revolution lasted 10 years.

Many heroic leaders continued to work for fairness and equality. Benito Juarez was a 19th-century president admired for his commitment to improving Mexico. Pancho Villa and Emiliano Zapata were revolutionaries who championed greater rights for poor and Mesoamerican people. Their passionate actions are remembered by many Mexicans.

Mario Molina is a modern-day hero and the first Mexican scientist to receive a Nobel Prize in chemistry.

11

SPIRITUAL LIFE AND LEGENDS

Each pre-Hispanic culture had its own religion. Important gods represented natural elements, and there were special ways to worship them and ask for help. Some Mesoamerican religions are still practiced on their own today, but most are creatively combined with Roman Catholicism. About 85 percent of Mexicans are Roman Catholic. This influences holidays, traditions, and everyday practices.

The story of Saint Juan Diego, a Mesoamerican peasant, is **commemorated** by Mexicans yearly on December 12. Stories say that, in 1531, the Virgin Mary appeared to Diego on a hill outside Mexico City and asked him to ensure a chapel was built in her honor nearby. Like many Mexicans, she had dark skin and spoke a Mesoamerican language. The Virgin of Guadalupe is an important symbol of Mexican faith. She represents the joining together of old and new religious beliefs. Her likeness is proudly displayed throughout the country.

Many Mexicans make special journeys, or pilgrimages, to visit a **basilica** built in honor of the Virgin of Guadalupe.

The Eagle and the Snake

The symbol on the Mexican flag comes from an Aztec legend. The Aztecs were **nomadic**, searching for a place to settle. According to a **prophecy**, the location they were looking for would be marked by an eagle sitting on a cactus eating a snake. When they finally found this sign in the center of a lake, they built the great city of Tenochtitlán on a system of floating gardens. This later became Mexico City, the largest city in the country and the longest continually occupied city in North America.

13

FESTIVALS AND FIESTAS

Mexican holidays are a lively mix of the Catholic calendar, Mesoamerican traditions, and national pride. Family holidays, such as birthdays, are observed with gatherings and meals. National holidays, such as Independence Day, are celebrated as a community with parades and parties. Religious holidays are celebrated with ritual foods and activities.

The Día de los Muertos, or Day of the Dead, is celebrated each November. This is when Mexicans invite the dead to rejoin them on Earth. A feast of favorite foods of the dead is prepared and laid out on an elaborate altar with bright yellow marigolds, decorative skulls made from sugar, photographs, and gifts. Some families stay overnight in the cemetery. They light candles, sing songs, pray, and eat together as a way of sharing a meal with their loved ones who have passed.

For Day of the Dead celebrations, bakers sell *pan de muerto,* or bread of the dead. This bread is sweetened with dried fruit and decorated with bone or skull shapes.

TRADITIONAL CUISINE

Mexican cuisine is known for its spicy and flavorful combinations. The core foods of beans, corn, and chilies have been eaten in Mexico since pre-Hispanic times. Chocolate, potatoes, and tomatoes are staples of Mesoamerican cuisine, which Mexicans still enjoy today.

There are over 100 kinds of Mexican chilies, or hot peppers. They come in many shapes, sizes, and degrees of spiciness, and they are fundamental to the taste of local dishes.

Spices and herbs such as cinnamon, cloves, cumin, thyme, oregano, and cilantro are also used to flavor dishes. Chocolate was a favorite treat of the Aztecs and is used in traditional recipes and special sauces. Some unusual ingredients such as crickets, insect eggs, and cactus also find a spotlight on the Mexican plate.

A woman in Cobá, Mexico, shapes tortillas with her hands in the traditional way. The tortillas are then cooked on a large, flat stone over a wood fire.

MEXICAN MASTERPIECES

Mexican art is often recognized for its vivid colors and lively scenes. People of the ancient civilizations created impressive pyramids, sculptures, and murals that provide clues to their daily life. Murals are the most recognizable Mexican art form, and Diego Rivera is one of the country's best-known muralists. His large wall paintings were commissioned for public buildings in the 1920s in Mexico as well as in the United States. They told the story of the Mexican people and drew together Mesoamerican and Spanish roots in historical scenes.

Frida Kahlo is the most famous Mexican artist in the world. She was married to Rivera. She painted self-portraits that explored her life story and identity as a woman and a Mexican. The bright colors, simple style, and even the clothing she wore were a tribute to Mesoamerican culture.

This large mural was painted by Diego Rivera. It tells the story of Mexico's history and can be seen by visitors at the National Palace in Mexico City.

Handcrafts

Handcrafts and folk art play an important role in the rich variety of Mexican life. People in different regions of Mexico specialize in crafts and trades such as pottery, weaving, jewelry making, leatherworking, woodworking, and basketry. Many of these crafts are both functional and decorative. For example, artists make beautiful pots that feature bright colors and flower designs. These pots can be used for cooking and serving food. Often, handcrafts are taught in schools and showcase the Mexican enthusiasm for color and tradition.

STORIES AND SYMBOLS

The earliest writing in Mexico used pictographs, or symbolic illustrations of words and ideas. Ancient people recorded important events by drawing pictographs on long, folded sheets of leather, cloth, or paper. Other Mesoamerican stories and poems were told from memory and preserved through storytelling. Many were later translated and printed in books by the Spanish.

Today, 95 percent of Mexicans speak Spanish, and most Mexican literature is written in Spanish. One of the most famous Mexican writers is Nobel Prize winner Octavio Paz. He wrote poetry and essays that explored Mexican life, myths, and culture.

For many years, much of Mexican literature centered around the Mexican Revolution. Later, patriotism became a popular theme. Mexican literature is well known and respected by people around the world.

A book made from ancient pictographs is called a codex. This is a copy of a codex that was created to record regular celebrations in the Aztec year.

The Writings of Sor Juana

Sor Juana Inés de la Cruz was born in 1651 near Mexico City. As a teenager, Sor Juana became a Catholic nun so she could read, write, and study freely. She wrote clever essays, plays, and poems. Although it was unusual at the time, Sor Juana believed that girls should go to school like boys. She used her writing to convince others that women had the right to be educated. A portrait of Sor Juana is featured on Mexican money.

TRADITIONAL CLOTHING

Alongside modern styles, traditional clothing is worn throughout Mexico. Blouses, wraparound skirts, and shawls, or wraps, are woven from dyed wool and cotton thread and decorated with detailed embroidery. Patterns change from village to village, so people may know where someone is from based on the design of their clothing.

Women choose traditional fashion more often than men. One exception in the guayabera, a type of shirt, which is still worn by men in Yucatán and Veracruz. Many women wear a huipil, which is a long tunic with an embroidered design. For festivals in central Mexico, it's common to see the china poblana. This is a style for women that combines a white blouse with a full, shiny red-and-green skirt. Men dress in clothing inspired by charros, or Mexican cowboys, for special occasions. They wear fitted jackets and pants with embroidered designs and gleaming buttons. Their wide hats are called sombreros.

A backstrap loom allows this woman to work outside and weave a traditional huipil.

Weaving

Women in Mexico create traditional clothing with time and skill. Natural dyes, such as blue from indigo plants and red from the cochineal insect, have made Mexican clothing vibrant for centuries. Once cotton or wool has been dyed and spun, it's ready to be woven on a loom. Many women use a portable backstrap loom. One end fits around the woman's back, and her body creates a tight frame for weaving. The woven cloth is sewn into garments.

23

ROUSING RHYTHMS

Small, ancient carvings of cheerful musicians tell us that music has always been important in Mexican life. Today, Mexican music and dance display a diverse cultural **heritage**, mixing different cultural styles. Many traditional dances across Mexico are set to music. They tell stories using energetic rhythms and movements and colorful, eye-catching costumes.

Mariachi, a traditional music style, is very popular. It is a symbol of Mexican culture. Mariachi bands perform in public places, such as the central square of a city. There, listeners can dance along and request their favorite songs. Guitars, violins, and trumpets are played by musicians wearing festive charro suits and sombreros. Themes of the songs include love, patriotism, and the revolution.

Today, traditional dances are performed at festivals such as the International Mariachi and Charros Festival in Guadalajara.

Traditional Dances

The music and costumes in a traditional dance give clues to where it came from. The Danza del Venado, or the Deer Dance, comes from the Yaqui and Mayo tribes and features a deer hunt. The Iguana, a dance from Guerrero, copies the movements of an iguana. The national dance of Mexico is a couple's dance called the Jarape Tapatío. Each dance has a **unique** message and reveals a different point of view in Mexican culture.

25

SPORTS AND GAMES

One of the world's oldest sports has its roots in Mexico. For thousands of years, Mesoamerican peoples played a ballgame that is similar to *fútbol*, also called soccer. Two groups competed to get a rubber ball past the other team and into a stone hoop. The players used their hips to pass the ball. The players were often warriors who participated to build their strength. Sometimes, the game was part of a special religious ritual.

Traditional Mexican sports also include bullfighting and *charreadas*, or rodeos. A style of wrestling called *lucha libre* is popular in Mexico. *Lucha libre* fans fill large, packed arenas to cheer on wrestlers. The matches have been rehearsed and the wrestlers are more like characters than athletes, with over-the-top costumes and names.

The Great Ball Court of Chichén Itzá is an ancient Mayan site in Yucatán, Mexico. In the game played here, teams of seven scored by sending heavy balls through stone hoops on the court walls.

SHARING MEXICAN CULTURE

Mexicans have been living in the United States for hundreds of years. Mexican Americans make up about 11 percent of the U.S. population. They bring with them their loyalty to family and community and their unique customs and celebrations. Many Mexican American communities are close-knit, supporting each other, speaking Spanish together, and honoring their heritage.

Mexican traditions can be seen everywhere in the United States. For example, many Mexican Americans throw quinceañera parties. A quinceañera is the celebration of a girl's 15th birthday. Another example can be found in Brownsville, Texas, where people come together to celebrate a Charro Days Fiesta. The Charro Days Fiesta is a chance for Mexican Americans to share stories about their past and celebrate their cultural identity. By continuing to practice old rituals and create new traditions, Mexican Americans celebrate their binational culture.

Day of the Dead celebrations have become very popular in the United States.

A CHANGING IDENTITY

Life in Mexico has changed significantly from pre-Hispanic times to the present day. Throughout history, Mexicans have found creative ways of adapting to modern life while preserving a unique identity. At times when their customs were threatened, Mexicans held onto the heart of old beliefs while combining them with new ones. As Mexico faces future challenges and welcomes new advances, there will be more opportunities to define what it means to be Mexican.

To look at Mexican culture is to appreciate the many ways that life can be lived, understood, and celebrated. Mexican traditions are inspiring, exciting, colorful, familiar, and sometimes mysterious. Observing them can improve our understanding of what it means to be part of a diverse and constantly changing world.

GLOSSARY

basilica: A large church that has a long central part that ends in a curved wall.

biodiversity: The variety of plants and animals that lives in an area or habitat.

commemorate: To remember officially.

custom: An action or way of behaving that is traditional among the people in a certain group or place.

deforestation: The act or result of cutting down or burning all the trees in an area.

diverse: Having many different kinds or varieties.

environment: The natural world around us.

heritage: The traditions and beliefs that are part of the history of a group or nation.

Mesoamerican: Of or relating to the southern part of North America and Central America that was—at one time—occupied by people with shared cultural features, such as the Maya and Aztecs.

migration: The movement of animals from one place to another as the seasons change.

nomadic: Having no fixed home and wandering from place to place.

pre-Hispanic: Of or relating to the cultures in North, Central, and South America before the arrival of the Spanish.

prophecy: A prediction of what's to come in the future.

ritual: A religious ceremony, especially one consisting of a series of actions performed in a certain order.

sacrifice: The act of offering up a gift as part of a religious ceremony, or the gift being offered.

unique: Being the only one of its kind.

INDEX

WEBSITES

Due to the changing nature of Internet links, PowerKids Press has developed an online list of websites related to the subject of this book. This site is updated regularly. Please use this link to access the list: www.powerkidslinks.com/chd/mexi